🎵 If Life is a song and we are born
with the lyrics,
then it is up to us to create
The music that fits.....

Michelle Cooke.

Dear Reader,

We all deserve the right to be happy and live happy lives. Unfortunately there is no step- by -step guide to happiness; it's a choice that only we can make. You can choose to live and strive for happiness on a daily basis or you can let others decide it for you. If you leave it to others you may miss out on the opportunity to have the life you really want. Don't let someone else navigate your life choices, don't let circumstances dictate the direction you want to go in and don't let your environment make decisions for you. If happiness is a part of your life plan (and I hope it is!) then please take the time to find out what your happiness feels and looks like. In this book I will share some memorable experiences and emotions that challenged me but also helped shape the person who I am today. On my road to finding my happiness I had ups and downs, like many others but during my journey I also learned a lot of valuable lessons. It is important that you understand that as you grow and develop into the person you wish to become you will make mistakes (or 'bad judgments' as I call them) but the important thing about these 'bad judgments' is to realise that you can actually learn from them.

As we grow we learn because it's what we were born to do.

I am the person I am today because I decided a very long time ago to seek out the opportunities each day to be happy and so can you. I hope this book will give you a helping hand in discovering the benefits of positive thinking and truly believing in yourself both INSIDE and OUT!!!

Be happy and stay blessed,

Michelle x

'Happiness resides not in possessions and not in Gold; the feeling of happiness dwells in the soul'

Democritus (Ancient Philosopher C460-370BC)

Contents

Introduction
Life purpose

From the moment you were born you were a special gift, someone worth knowing and loving. You were born for a purpose and nobody can tell you what your purpose is. Not your parents, your friends or even your teachers can tell you because it is something you will discover over time. When you took your first step, said your first word, rode your bike for the first time and even on your first day at School you were on the road to Independence. You create milestones and moments which collectively help shape who you are. As you get older and begin to discover who you are you will continue to create more and more milestones which will then help shape the person you will become.

There may be a time in your life where you find yourself asking the question "why am I here?" it may seem like a rather spiritual question but it's one that only you can answer. I think the important thing to do if/when the question ever pops up is to use it to evaluate what you're doing, feeling and thinking at that moment and decide whether those actions, thoughts and feelings fit in with what you want out of life. More importantly the question may help you decide if they actually coincide with person you want to be. I always use 'who am I?' as the question to establish whether or not I am on the right track. The answer then leads to an area of self discovery.

I would imagine that some of the most successful people you know have given some thought to their life purpose at least once! Do you have a favorite celebrity at the moment? An actor/actress, a Singer, maybe it's a rapper, someone in your family, community or even Church? I bet they would be able to tell you with no hesitation what their life purpose is and this is because they dared to ask and discover. They are who they are today because of it believe me!! But as I said earlier the answer to the question is a personal one and only you can answer it. It doesn't even matter if you ask yourself the question more than once and your answer is different each time. You ask, you discover, you then take the required actions to BE!

If you're sitting there thinking "what a load of rubbish" or simply don't believe or understand the notion of having a purpose, that's ok. Just because we don't believe or understand something doesn't mean we can't discover it. A lot of us don't understand electricity but we use and benefit from it every day. If you're still not convinced then

I guess what I am saying and about to say won't make a bit of difference to you but I hope you will humor me for a little longer and continue to read on. If you want to discover your life purpose you must first believe and be open to the idea that you do indeed have one. So to get started! I want you to Get a blank piece of paper and a pen and start with the writing the heading 'why am I here?' then I want you to write whatever comes into your head. Think of all the things you are good at and enjoy doing. You may start by writing something funny or ridiculous but keep writing until the answers have meaning and become almost emotional. I guarantee you'll find the clue to your answer. Keep repeating this until you come up with an answer that triggers happy feelings. You're then on the right track!

When I was at college studying a Business Diploma I had a wonderful lecturer who I will never forget. He was a short rather plump man with a strong American accent. He had a great sense of humor and a unique style of teaching which made his lessons all the more interesting. He took the time to get to know his students unlike the other lecturers and this made him very popular, especially with the girls. Anyway, I remember we had an important assignment which was to create our own companies from scratch which meant we would have to come up with an idea, do market research, profit and loss summaries, find our target groups etc. This was an important part of the course as the grade went towards our final over-all mark. Everyone was really excited. I noticed a lot of the girls in the group had decided to set up businesses that were a little too predictable for me, you know Hair Salons (not knocking hairdressers I know I couldn't survive without mine!!), Nursery's, tanning salons and Clothing Boutiques. The boy's idea's ranged from Motorbike shops, Computer shops and an Electricians company. I remember one of the boys even decided on a funeral parlor for his business.... Hmmm nice!!!! I really wanted to set up a business that was realistic and more in tune with who I was and that's what made the decision so hard. So I decided to talk to the lecturer about it. I explained that I wanted to come up with an idea that would make a good viable business but had no clue as to what that could be. His advice to me was to go home and make a list of my goals and the things I wanted to achieve. At that point I was confused. I really didn't see how this was going to help. Not only that but it sounded like extra home work and that did not entertain me at all. Nevertheless I went home and thought about what he had said. I stared at a blank piece of paper for what felt like hours. I managed to write the word "GOALS" at the top of the page but after that my mind went blank and I became increasingly frustrated. Why didn't I just opt for a hairdressing salon? After a further hour of thinking my list began. It started off slow and then before I knew it I had come up with the following;

1...I want to earn enough money to pay all my Mom's bills so she doesn't have to work.

2...I want to travel and meet interesting people

3...I want to be able to help people and get paid for it

4...I want everyone around me to be happy and live happy stress- free lives

5...I want to be rich

6...I want a BMW

7...I want to own a successful Business and employ people so I can take time off and I can travel

8...I want my own TV show like Oprah Winfrey

Those were my goals and things I wanted to achieve the most. I wasn't sure how this was going to help but I was interested in finding out. The next day I gave the lecturer my list and waited for an explanation. He sat there looking at the piece of paper whilst stroking his beard. He then wrote a message on it in red ink and handed it back to me. The message read; *now think of a business that would enable you to achieve your goals.* Then he explained that by coming up with an idea that best suited me and one that I felt passionately about would enable me to get the grade I wanted. It may also give me a clearer picture of what type of business I wanted to set up and what would be involved once I had left college. I instantly saw the logic behind this and decided to go home and give it some serious thought. Unfortunately an idea didn't come to me straight away, in fact it wasn't until two days later in the very early hours of the morning the idea hit me; a Medical Health Centre!! But not your everyday Health centre, more like a wellbeing centre that housed a variety of Therapists. I wanted it to be more about holistic therapy than medicine, a place where people could go for Hypnotherapy, Counseling, personal development and even parenting classes. I think my idea was inspired by my old Doctor. I had seen him a few days before. He had been my Doctor for over 12 years before he retired. He had told me that he was treating private patients from his home. He had decided to work with patients that had mental health issues as opposed to medical issues. I wasn't sure what that involved but he made it sound good and I was ever so impressed. He had always showed my mom and me a lot of respect. He was a great Doctor and his new business venture sounded like something I would be interested in. The more and more I thought about it the more excited I became. This is how I knew I was on to something and I just had to follow it through. So, with my list of goals and my new found inspiration, my ideas were at last in operation. The weeks that followed involved lots of research and complete dedication. Within a few days I had contacted the Doctor who happily gave me the information and advice that I needed and researched what it would take to set up the business I had in mind. I was 100% committed to the assignment and felt so good doing it that it didn't feel like work.

Three weeks and a day later my assignment was complete. Everyone was surprised at my choice of business but extremely impressed with the amount of effort I had put in. I am happy to say that I received a Distinction for that particular assignment...... that was a relief! Reflecting on my goals and giving a little thought to what I wanted to achieve had actually paid off, who knew?

Now you're probably expecting me to say that I am now the proud owner of a successful Medical Health Centre, I drive a BMW and that I have achieved every single one of the Goals on my list. Sorry to disappoint you but I'm not quite there yet, Oprah has not yet called and my list has changed slightly over the years. I am, however a qualified Stress Consultant, Cognitive Therapist and Life Coach which means that I help people overcome some of the mental obstacles that prevent them from living happy lives. It took me almost 10 years of re- writing and analysing my' goal list plus a string of unsuccessful business start-ups to realise that my purpose is and always has been to help others. I guess I had never really tried to discover my 'purpose' until that assignment but I'm glad I did. It's ironic really because friends would always come to me with their problems or for advice they used to call me 'miss agony aunt' or 'the problem solver'. I strongly believe that we are all born for a reason and that we are all here to add value to our families, friends and even the world.

Why not try......

A life purpose questionnaire:

Write your answers on a piece of paper.

1) What makes you smile and feel good?   (Activities, people, events, etc)

2) What were the things you enjoyed doing when you were younger?

3) What things do you enjoy doing now?

4) Is there an activity you enjoy doing that makes you lose track of time?

5) Who inspires you?

6) What makes you feel good about yourself?

7) What are your natural talents or what do others notice you're good at?

8) Do people ask for your help? What sort of things do they ask of you?

9) If you had the opportunity to teach something what would it be?

10) Imagine you were much older (say 70 years old) reflecting on your life and how wonderful and blessed your life has been. What would your memories be?

Give the questionnaire a try and see what you come up with! You may be surprised with the feelings you evoke by participating. You can use the questionnaire more than once. It may help you realise your purpose or give you some goals to strive for.

'How can you tell me that the sky is the limit when people are flying to the moon'

Motivation

Have you ever seen people jogging along the roadside or around the park really early in the morning or very late at night? It could be raining, snowing or the hottest day in June. Is your first thought "why?" or "are they crazy?" Obviously they must have their reasons, right? There must be some kind of motivation I mean, why else would they be doing it? Maybe they want to get into shape for a holiday or maybe they do it to relieve some kind of stress. Whatever the reason maybe it's something that is important to them. They have their motivation and the will power and they seem to block out any distractions and stay focused.

I remember when I was at school. One of my favorite subjects was P.E. I loved any form of physical activity. Once a year the school would have a sports day event and this took place on the fields that surrounded the school grounds. For me it was the opportunity to compete against my fellow classmates and it was also a day without lessons. Every year without fail I would enter the long distance running race. This year in particular was extremely important as I really needed to win. The year before I had come joint first and the year before that I came in second place. The funny thing about it was that my biggest competitor was always the same girl. Since this was our final year I just had to win. I don't know about you but I am a terrible loser. I needed to show my classmates and the rest of the school how good I was. So I decided the best way to prepare myself for the challenge was to go into training and focus on winning. I didn't want anyone to know that I was worried about the race so I trained in secret. I ran everywhere. I ran to school, home from school, up and down the stairs and when it wasn't convenient to run around I ran on the spot and it did my mom's head in! I never kept still for a second. I can remember losing sleep because I just couldn't wait for the big day.

When the day had finally arrived I was so anxious and full of adrenaline. Standing at the starting line and looking at the crowd made me feel sick. Everyone around me seemed so relaxed and calm but I was the opposite. Whilst I waited for the race to start I decided it would be a good idea to warm up, like they do in the Olympics. I reenacted every breathing and stretching technique I had seen on TV and it felt good. I did notice a few people laughing at me and yes thinking back I must have looked really silly but you have to understand I wanted to win more than anything so them mocking me made me even more determined. We were told to get into our starting positions and I kept my thoughts firmly fixed on the finishing line. The horn sounded and we were off. I ran my little heart out. I remember my competitor and I being neck and neck for the first part of the race but there was no way I was letting her win or settling for joint first place again. That's when it happened, I saw her feet "NO NO" I yelled. I wasn't going to let this happen. I told myself that my baby brother had been kidnapped and the only way I was going to save him was to win the race. I imagined how upset my mom would be if I lost the race and we never saw my brother again so I ran faster and harder. With anger in my belly and tears in my eyes I let out an almighty scream I ran so fast I thought my legs were going to fall off. At one stage I even felt my feet hitting my backside. With my head held high and the sound of cheering echoing in my ears I ran like a girl possessed. The cheering got louder and louder then they suddenly turned into laughter. I wasn't sure what was happening so I decided to look around. To my surprise there was no one behind me. I quickly realised that I had run past the finishing line and on my way to running another lap. How embarrassing!! I hate feeling embarrassed so I decided to do a few cartwheels and a funny dance to try and give the impression that I had done it on purpose. Not sure if it worked but I didn't care. All my friends ran towards me cheering and laughing. I had won the race!! That is a day I will never forget and one I often reflect on when I am setting myself new challenges.

I think it's important to set yourself goals no matter how small they seem. To some of you winning a race may appear a rather small goal but to me it meant a lot. If I compare it to some of the goals I have set myself since then you may have a point but it was something that motivated me. I was passionate and I saw it through until the end and I never gave up and that's what's important. Motivation has come to me in different ways. For example; I have a very dear friend who a few years ago was shot and nearly lost his life. He was the victim of a robbery that went terribly wrong and as a result he had a stroke and lost the use of his right arm and leg. He was told he may never walk again without the aid of a wheelchair or a walking stick. But during his recovery stage he decided he would walk and become the man he was before the incident. He remained motivated every single day despite the Doctors warnings. He never gave up on the idea of walking. He gave himself twelve months to recover and every day until then remained focused. Even though it took him sixteen months in total to regain his strength, he did achieve his goal. Now he is a mentor and travels the country giving talks to young adults on the dangers of gun crime. He has also set up a creative arts organisation for young adults at risk of offending and is doing really well. Not only is he an inspiration to me and others but he is also motivating.

What motivates you? Think about it for a few minutes. Maybe there is something you want to achieve within the next six to twelve months. Do you want to save enough money to buy a loved one a gift? Do you wish to join a club or take up a hobby? Whatever it is write it down and put it where you can see it. Everyday actively do the things you need to do to help achieve it.

Why not try……

- Make a list of your goals. Find a major goal from your list.

- Complete what you start. It is very important you get into the habit of doing this.

- Talk to other people who have the same or similar interest to you.

- Seek out people who motivate and support your goal(s)

- Constantly tell yourself that you WILL achieve your goals despite fear.

- Visualise your goal, every detail of it and never loose focus.

- Don't procrastinate!!! It leads to laziness and laziness leads to nothing.

FEAR!

Fear can often stop us from achieving our goals and reduce our motivation. It can prevent us from having new experiences, meeting people and embarking on new adventures. It is important to realise that everything we feel begins in the mind. If you think about losing then you've already lost!

I admit that I have given into fear quite a few times. This was before I took the time to understand and control it. I decided to change the way I interpret it because my problem was the fear of failing. It pretty much came out of nowhere and would stop me in my tracks. Instead of simply doing the things I wanted and needed to do I began asking myself 'what if?' I would come face- to- face with a situation and let fear be my primary decision maker. Instead of thinking about the possibilities of actually doing the thing I was afraid of I would concentrate on the 'what if it goes wrong' or 'what if I don't succeed' type of questions.

A prime example of this came shortly after I left college. I had decided to take a year off studying so I could work and earn money to pay for driving lessons. I applied for every job going but I had no joy. I was either inexperienced or too young it was frustrating and deflating. Then one day my Mom came home from work looking like she had just won the lottery (I wish she had because then I wouldn't of needed a job!) She had found out that there was a clerical position vacant at her work place. The idea didn't thrill me but I agreed to apply. Within a few short days they called me with an interview date. At that point I was fine but that was until I received the confirmation letter with a detailed description of what would be expected of me if I were to get the job. I was prepared for the odd bit of filing, answering the phones and typing but I wasn't at all prepared for the end of the month target presentations or the fact that I would be pretty much thrown into the deep end and expected to cover other members of staff whilst they went on their breaks. I was sure I wouldn't get the job as I had no prior experience in an office let alone doing presentations in front of people I didn't know. My stomach was in knots and I knew I couldn't discuss it with my Mom. She would have given her "Oh stop worrying about it" or "stop being silly!" response and whilst those are meant as words of encouragement I didn't want to hear it. I really wanted a job but the fear of failing just wouldn't go away. To cut a long story short I made up an excuse and cancelled my interview and ended up working in a factory.

The money wasn't great but it was a job. Around six months later my Mom and I bumped into the girl who got the job I had applied. She explained how she had moved to a different department, undergone training and had been given a company car. Was I gutted? Yep! Not only had I missed out on the opportunity to earn more money than I was currently earning but also the opportunity to get a company car and since I had just past my driving test that bit of news was like a slap in the face with a wet fish!

Unfortunately for me that was the first of many missed opportunities. My fears had prevented me from all types of experiences such as networking, holidays, having relationships and gaining employment. As I said, I had to completely change my thought process so that I could discover my true life purpose and be happy. Fear was never and will never be a friend of mine!! Below is a simple but effective breakdown of what fear actually is:

FALSE

EXPECTATIONS

APPEARING

REAL

If fear is something you can relate to then you too should actively find ways of overcoming it. If change is what you want (and I hope it is) seek it and be happy. There are also people you can discuss your fears with either professionals (try you're GP) or a family member. Talk to someone who has your best interests at heart

Why not try......

In the face of fear have what I call *self conversations.*
Instead of focusing on the "what if'" focus on the "why"
instead. For example; your about to take your driving test
and you worry about how you will feel if you don't pass
and you begin to embrace the feelings of failing. **STOP!**
Replace those feelings of failure with the feelings you
would get if you were to pass. Take a moment to reflect on
the reasons why you're taking the test in the first place.
Imagine you have passed your test and you're now
independent. No more asking your Mom and Dad for a lift
or waiting at the bus stop watching everyone drive by.
You can now go places you have always wanted to go.
Think of all that freedom!!

Let's say you have a job interview and fear kicks in. Those
horrible feelings of doubt dominate your thoughts again, I
want you to concentrate on why you applied for the job in
the first place. Let the "why?" take over. Think of how
having that job will benefit your life and how happy you
will be once you're working and **financially** independent.

If you begin to feel fear creeping up on you, why not try
some deep breathing. Find a quiet place to sit. Sit in an
upright position with your eyes closed. Take long deep
breaths in and then breathe out slowly. While your

breathing out focus on the 'why'. Repeat this 5-6 times and relax.

'Our greatest weakness lies in giving up.

The most certain way to succeed is to always try one more time '

Thomas Edison (American inventor 1847-1931)

 **Relationships**

Having a relationship with yourself....

What kind of relationship do you have with your friends? What about your parents? Do you have a partner? How is that relationship? Good or Bad? I imagine you have no problem answering those questions. Now, here's a question that might take you a little longer to answer. What kind of relationship do you have with yourself? Yes, you read right, yourself! I know at first it may seem like a stupid question and one you may find difficult to comprehend but it is indeed a genuine one and one I want you to think about. Before any of us can have a meaningful relationship with others it is vital to place some attention to the relationship we have with ourselves.

    We all tend to attract the things, the situations and even the people based on how we think and feel. Negative feelings can come from the beliefs and judgments we make about life. It is necessary to pay attention to these feelings. We must think long and hard as to whether they are ones that are keeping us on the right path to who we want to be. Ask yourself whether these beliefs you are holding are actually your own or ones you have adopted from your friends, family, your partner or even your teachers. Ask yourself if your life would be any different if you were to think differently about these beliefs. Would your judgments change? How would you feel about yourself? Would you like or love yourself more or less? Do you think you're the type of person who is capable of loving yourself as much as you love others? Do you feel open to the idea that by choosing to love yourself you chose to achieve more successful and positive relationships with others? Your probably wondering why all the questions? Believe me by questioning yourself and assessing the answers you will get to know yourself on a deeper level and find out what really makes you tick.

As infants our first instinct is to take care of ourselves. We place our needs before others in fact we demand it! However as we grow older those behaviors are considered selfish so we are reconditioned with the idea that we must put others before ourselves. In order for you to really get to know yourself you must first look beyond your *exterior* such as your facial features, hair color, eye color, age, sex etc and get in touch with your *interior* i.e. your thoughts, feelings and your reactions. Secondly you must learn to listen to yourself and I mean stop everything and listen. Spend a few minutes or longer by yourself. Quiet time will give you the opportunity to really think about your feelings and actions. It will give you the opportunity to assess you're thinking process, your decisions and your behaviors. By doing this you begin to take better care of *YOU*. If this doesn't sound like something that would work for you then may I suggest you try writing down what you're thinking and feeling each day and evaluate them. If this works then continue this method until you're comfortable with dealing with your thoughts and feelings internally.

Our daily routines often leave us neglecting what we really feel. So how do we know if we are on the right track? This is why I strongly recommend you take the time to discover what is best for you. Getting to know yourself on a deeper level has its advantages. You will........

....begin to treat yourself better

....get along with people better

....attract the kind of people who will treat you as well as they see you treat yourself

....realise that negative self talk has a negative impact on your life

....realise that thinking about your best interests and what makes you happy is not selfish.

Now don't get me wrong I didn't wake up one morning shouting "hello self how are you today and by the way I love you!" No, it was more along the lines of "why do I feel so low?" I began questioning myself regularly. I seemed to attract negative relationships that left me feeling unworthy, ugly, lonely and often depressed. So I decided to control the situations that occurred in my life rather than them controlling me. I started by asking myself "how can I change these results?" I had to find out what it was I was doing wrong.

Have you ever found yourself in a situation that just doesn't feel right? Your gut instinct tells you to run a mile but you ignore it? This is a classic reaction that I call *ignoring yourself.* I know it may sound a little bizarre but that's exactly what it is and we all do it. I did it so many times that it became second nature. The more I refused to listen to myself the more I hated myself for doing so. A prime example of this was the time I fell in love with a compulsive cheat. I knew of his reputation with the ladies and should have known better. My first instinct was to run as far away as possible but he was so charming and extremely good looking. It was like I felt almost privileged that he wanted to be with me.

The first three months were great and I was on cloud nine. That cloud soon turned to rain when I found out he was cheating on me. Of course I broke it off and I should have left it at that but I didn't. His constant calls and apologies won me over and I eventually gave in. He promised he would never cheat again and although the voice in my head was saying "NO, NO" I didn't listen. I went straight back like a fly to pooh! I convinced myself that I was the one that needed to change to prevent him from doing it again. Even though I did everything I could to make him happy I failed to recognise that I was making myself miserable. It wasn't long before he cheated again but the difference this time was that the girl he cheated on me with became pregnant and I found out that piece of information from someone else. I ended the relationship, changed my number and spent many months depressed and angry at the fact that I hadn't listen to myself in the first place. I remember having a conversation with a friend shortly after the break up. I cried a lot, she listened and said all the things that friends say when you're low and upset but there was one thing she said that I will never forget because it was this that which inspired me to really think about the way I treated myself, she said" Michelle I love you to bits but why don't you start taking a dose of your own medicine? You always see the best in people and you treat them better than you treat yourself. Now you should start seeing the best in yourself'. I remember being silent for a few minutes and for once I was speechless. She had definitely given me something to think about and that is exactly what I did. The funny thing about it was that she didn't tell me anything that I hadn't already said to myself. If only I had listened it would have saved me months of heartache. Luckily for me I was still young and had time the time to learn from my bad judgment.

You'll be surprised how negative relationships with others can really wear you down and have a damaging effect on the relationship you have with yourself. I think that all of the negative relationships and situations I encountered did me a favor. By reflecting on my past and reviewing all the 'bad judgments' I had made helped me realise I wasn't being a good friend to myself at all. I spent years searching for my true happiness; unfortunately I was looking in the wrong places. I relied on family, friends and sometimes even people I didn't know that well at all to show me who I was and what I was worth which is like looking in the fridge for ice cubes......*pointless!!*

There are people who live their whole lives not really getting to know themselves at all. They live in a world dominated by others thoughts, opinions and actions. They miss out on their true happiness and ultimately finding their life purpose. Could you imagine living with someone for eighty years and being totally ignored? They don't listen to anything you say even when what you're trying to say protects them from harm. How would you feel? Well, this is what we are theoretically doing when we fail to listen to ourselves. This brings me back to the point I made earlier about becoming reconditioned as infants, that we are somehow selfish if we place priority on how we feel. Being in tune with yourself doesn't mean you can't be thoughtful, caring, understanding and loving towards others. It simply means that you relate to others in a positive, caring and considerate way and attract the situations that make you happy. Whether you're a boy or a girl reading this right now, trust me, it's important for you to understand the importance of listening to your inner voice! That voice will become your best friend.

I LOVE ME....

Life is what you make it or so the saying goes

But do I have to live it with these ears, this bum, and these toes?

"You're beautiful as you are" is what my Mom keeps telling me

She's say's I look just like her Aunt

Great I say, she's 53

I want to be a Model NO! an Actress on TV

Or

I could be a rapper and duet with Jay Z

My Teacher say's I'm lazy and need to buck up my ideas

My friends think I am funny and I have them all in tears

If I don't become a Model or an actress on TV or I don't

Become a rapper and duet with Jay Z

I'll be happy with whatever I do

'cause that's how it should be,

it doesn't matter what people say

BECAUSE I LOVE ME!!!!!!!

Why not try......

Because listening to your self can be hard to do as we all have an awful lot of things going on. It is important to evaluate your thoughts and actions. Start by asking yourself the following;

1) When was the last time you did something for someone else? Did you do it just to make them happy?

2) Have you ever changed the way you look or dressed to please someone else even though it wasn't to your taste?

3) Have you ever said yes to something you really wanted to say no to?

If you have answered yes to any of the above questions think about how you felt. Were you happy? Did you feel proud, confident or did you feel lonely, depressed and full of dread? Once you have thought about this try clearing your mind of the situations and replace them with events that have left you feeling happy, positive and empowered.

Relationships cont......

'Whenever you're in conflict with someone, there is one factor that can make a difference between damaging your relationship and dampening it, that factor is attitude'

> William James (American Philosopher, 1842–1910)

Having a Relationship with others......

Relationships are important to us all. They add value to our lives especially if they are healthy and supportive. We will encounter a variety of relationships in our lifetime ranging from the ones we have with our family and friends to the one we experience at work, college or even at Church. All play a significant part in our lives, even the bad ones; this is because we learn from everyone we meet.

I had a friend called Suzanne while I was in secondary school. She was an absolute nutter! That was why I liked her we used to sit together in class everyday. We went on long bike rides to the Skate Park to watch the older kids do fascinating skateboarding tricks. On weekends we would have sleepovers and do fun stuff like trying on our moms clothes or raiding the fridge late at night when our parents were asleep. She was so much fun to be around but what we shared was more than humor and fun. We would talk for hours about all kinds of things ranging from Hair, make-up, music to ambitions. We shared our fears and what we wanted to be when we were older. We would even have discussions about our religious beliefs since she was a Catholic and I was raised a Christian. I can honestly say without a shadow of a doubt that she was my rock throughout the turbulent and often confusing times of adolescence. I saw the two of us as Soldiers surviving the unpredictable dangers life would throw at us. We relied on each other and we had a special relationship. It was the greatest feeling in the world to have her in my life. However, once we had left Secondary School our friendship slowly began to fade. She went to a different College to the one I went to and even though she was only the other side of town the bond we once shared had broken. We didn't part on bad terms but I guess we were only meant to be a part of each other's life for a short period of time and in that time a special friendship was made. I really believe that relationships should feel that way, don't get me wrong they can be hard work and complicated at times but healthy relationships help us grow. The not so healthy ones can be draining of our positive energies and should be avoided.

A close friend of mine has always had an amazing relationship with her mom. When we were kids I remember they would spend an awful lot of time together.

She wasn't an only child she had two younger brothers. She and her mother would do cool stuff together like go Roller Skating, go to the Cinema, go to the hairdressers and they would even spend evenings painting each other's nails and watching films, you know the sort of things you usually do with your friends! I just didn't get it I mean, I only went shopping and to the Hairdressers with my mom because I had no choice. My friend would come into School bragging about how much fun she had had with her Mom and too be honest it became a little bit annoying. The words 'mom' and 'fun' just didn't belong in the same sentence. I was at that stage in my life where I couldn't wait until I was old enough to leave home. When I was complaining about my Moms constant nagging, she would give me 'chapter and verse' about how she wasn't leaving home until she was at least twenty five because she was having so much fun. I was convinced at that point that she must have needed some sort of medication I mean, HELLO!? Who in their right mind would want to spend more time than they had to living with their parents? I'm not saying the relationship I had with my mom was a bad one because most of the time it was OK. I have rather fond memories of my mum and I having a laugh and spending quality time but those moments became very few and far between as I got older.

My mom is and always been a 'super organised' woman. Everything has to be done her way and exactly how she does it. As a single parent mother of two she was far too busy to do the fun things. We would argue a lot about her constant nit –picking as at one stage it seemed like nothing I did was good enough. I admit that sometimes I would give her a valid reason to complain but I felt at times she would create a fuss just because she could and not necessarily because she needed to. That was our relationship in a nutshell! Between the ages of ten and seventeen my mom and I did not see eye to eye at all. My teenage years consisted of bad moods, tantrums, door slamming, bedroom isolation and a lot of grounding (obviously I'm describing me and not my mom). But when I reflect on those years I can honestly say that as much as fun wasn't a top priority love definitely was. No matter what my Mom did or said or didn't do and didn't say I felt the love and this was something I didn't truly appreciate until I left home. Once I had left home I missed all the things I used to complain about and found myself doing the things I hated doing when I lived at home. It was then I became grateful for the way my mum displayed her love for me (even though at the time it drove me mad) I appreciated the reasons behind the curfews, the grounding and the 'nagging' and often find myself repeating the very same words to my own children. I have an amazing relationship with my mom now, she is my best friend.

The moral of this story is that when we refer to the word 'relationship' we often associate it with friends, boyfriends or girlfriends but never with our family members. Is this due to the fact that we subconsciously take those relationships for granted? Is it then acceptable for us to place less importance or priority on them?

If the relationship you're having with your parents is far from harmonious at the moment, try not to give them a hard time. Spend a little time reflecting on the positive aspects of your relationship. Remember that they were young once and have experienced all kinds of emotions and situations. Consider for a moment that no one is perfect and that love is always a parents' motivation behind the discipline, the boundaries and the curfews and not because they don't want you to have fun or to be happy.

One definition describes a relationship as; *a particular type of connection existing between people related or having dealings with each other.*

Healthy relationships take time to create. They offer us support, love and happiness. They are not only good for our moral but they are extremely beneficial to our health. They give us comfort in knowing someone is there come rain or shine and add value to our lives.

Why not try......

To establish whether the relationship you are in at the moment is a healthy one and right for who you are, ask yourself the following;

- Do you trust them? Trust makes the relationship stronger.

- Do you have respect for each other? If you respect them they will respect you and visa versa.

- Is your relationship an honest one? One without honesty cannot be real.

- Do they accept you for who you are? It's important they do not try and change you.

- Are they reliable? It's nice to have people around you that you can count upon. Through the good times and the bad.

- Do you appreciate one another? When you appreciate each other, communication becomes stress free.

- Do you laugh? How often? Laughing and having fun can add an awful lot to a relationship as they establish a connection. Laughter is also known as a great ice breaker after a disagreement!

- Healthy relationships are essential to our happiness and also our emotional health.

Stress

What is stress? We all interpret stress in different ways. This is because of the way we feel about it and its causes. Something that causes stress for me may not cause stress for you. It can be described as a buildup of pressure and anxiety. But stress on its own is not really harmful; too much of it however can have a profound effect on us. Believe it or not Stress can actually be a useful reaction. It can often give us the OOMPH we need to take a required action but this is only if the energy (the adrenaline) it causes is used. Its only when this energy is left to manifest within the mind and body its effects can be negative.

A lot of us are not actually aware of the effects that stress can actually have on our bodies. Our blood pressure and our heartbeat increases and our breathing becomes irregular. The hormone called adrenaline is then released into the bloodstream. This is our body's way of preparing us for action also known as the 'fight' or 'flight' response which is the bodies' automatic response to a perceived threat or danger. If the energy caused by the adrenaline is used the effects of stress can be quite positive. If the cause of the stress is not identified it can lead to all kinds of symptoms such as depression, anxiety, lack of concentration, anger and mood swings. Because we all respond differently to stress it's important we work out useful strategies to overcome its effects. By finding ways to overcome the effects we make the results of stress far less dramatic

My first real experience with stress occurred when I was just 17 years old shortly after I had given birth to my first child. I was still at college. I studied extremely hard and attended all my lessons. Within a three week period I had given birth to a beautiful baby girl and sat my exams. Even though my family seemed supportive I knew deep down they were disappointed in me. They had my future mapped out for me you see. My Mom thought I would go to College, then to university and after that I would get good job. Then of course I would meet Mr. Right, get married and have kids. As far as my family were concerned me having a baby at this age would prevent me from achieving my goals and dampen my dreams of becoming successful. I spent months trying hard to convince them that I could have a baby and a career to the point where I felt drained. I knew that with the right amount of support and determination that I could do it. I had faith in myself so why didn't they? Every day seemed like a battle. No matter how hard I tried to prove them all wrong I just couldn't get through to them.

The pressure of being a new mom and trying to live up to everyone's expectations left me in a complete state of physical and mental exhaustion No wonder I gave into stress and slipped into a mild state of depression. At first I put a brave face on it but that made it worse. Eventually I became disconnected from my friends, my appetite went, my optimistic attitude turned sour and crying was the only reaction I knew. The girl who never used to care about other people's opinions, that would be so focused and head strong had gone and I missed her. I wanted the old me back. When I looked in the mirror I hardly recognised myself I looked tired and almost life-less. My best friend tried everything she could to cheer me up bless her! But nothing worked. I was stressed and that was a fact. I had spent several months trying to brush it under the carpet and in the end I just didn't have the energy. But I knew I needed to change the way I was thinking in order to change the way I was feeling. And this was no easy task. With my exams results around the corner and a lifetime of responsibilities ahead I needed to get back to my old self again.

One evening I was tidying up my room and I came across an old pair of trainers my Dad had brought me. I remember I had bugged him for weeks to get them for me. I had blackmailed him into buying them for me as compensation for not spending as much time with me as he had promised. He was a Martial Arts Instructor in those days and if he wasn't taking part in tournaments he was training which meant I didn't see him much. Even when I did see him he was either at the gym or going for a run. When I asked him why he was always so active he explained how sometimes going for a run would help him clear his head. It gave him the opportunity to think especially if he was stressed or had a problem he needed to sort out. That's when it hit me! I enjoyed physical activities when I was younger and I was always happy when I was active so that night I decided that any opportunity I had I would go for a run. The idea excited me and I couldn't wait to get started.

Every day without fail I would either go for walks with the baby or go for a long run. Within a few months I started to feel a lot better and it showed. My negative thoughts had become positive ones and I noticed everybody responded to me differently. My mom eased up the pressure, my friends were around me more and my zest for life had returned. I had physically and mentally transformed. I past my exams and the future was once again looking bright. My new found confidences even lead me to apply to University. I began focusing on what I needed to do to make my life better rather than what I thought others expected of me

Some may say that I live a stressful life today; juggling my children, my career, my studies, and a social life. I'm often asked 'how do you do it?' Don't get me wrong my life involves a certain amount of pressure but I don't allow that pressure get the better of me. I exercise regularly; I eat good food and try to get a good night's sleep. I have also gotten into the habit of prioritising the things I need to do. For example if I have a busy week ahead or a deadline to meet, I make a list. I place the important things at the top of my list and work my way down and this enables me to get them out of the way and leaves my mind clear. I can then deal with the less important stuff later on. You know what it's like, you have something really important to do and you put it off to deal with the less important stuff first and what happens? You end up completely anxious and find it hard to focus and the important things becomes a problem that can often lead to stress.

As I have said before the things that I may find stressful you may not find stressful at all. It is something that we all respond to differently. This is why some stress is 'good' and some is 'bad'. I think the experience I had as a teenager was actually the 'good' stress as I found a way of coping (even though it didn't feel too good at the time) if I hadn't the effects could have been far worse. I rose to the challenge so to speak! Although I haven't experienced 'bad' stress in its entirety I have seen the effects of it.

When my Cousin announced he was going to University we were all so proud of him. He decided to live in the accommodation near the campus so he wouldn't have to commute. He was usually an outgoing and happy person but that slowly changed. On his visits home during the holidays his Mom had noticed the change. He had become withdrawn, moody, his enthusiasm had gone and he was losing weight. There was obviously something wrong but he refused to talk to any of us about it. Unfortunately he ended up having to leave University due to a break down. He couldn't handle the pressure of University and living away from home and this led to stress. He also felt too embarrassed to admit he was finding the experience too daunting. This is a classic example of what happens when the cause of the stress itself is not identified and therefore not dealt with effectively.

Why not try……

We will never live stress free lives, its impossible! No matter how hard we try stress will always be around us. Your stress could be related to school, home life, relationships, starting a new job etc whatever it is we simply can't avoid it. So here is a list of strategies to help make the effects of stress less traumatic and easier to cope with

- Communication: Try to communicate your feelings with your parents, a family member or friend.

- Eat well: Drink plenty of water. Avoid too much alcohol and caffeine.

- Plenty of rest: Get the recommended 8 hours a day sleep; situations can often appear worse when you're tired.

- Exercise: Going for a run, a jog or a long walk can help relax you and help you feel better about yourself.

- Prioritise: Take care of the important things that need to be done first.

- Stay positive: Get rid of negative thoughts

- Write it down: Keep a 'Stress' journal. This will help you draw attention to the stresses and also identify the causes, for example; I didn't meet the deadline for my assignment or I lost my Oyster Card etc also include how you actually dealt with the situations. Did you get upset, cry, and shout? Once you have recognised the cause of the stressors you will be in a better position to find manageable ways of coping.

- Take a break: Listening to music, talking to a friend. Reading or watching TV can be a nice distraction from a stressful situation.

- Don't take on too much: Deal with things a little bit at a time.

<u>Why not try some useful Breathing Techniques:</u>

Choose a time when the house is quiet;

Lie down and close your eyes, use a cushion or pillow to support your head. Whilst in the laying position, place your hand on your stomach just underneath your rib cage.

Breathe in slowly and deeply through your nose. Your stomach should rise pushing your hand up. Through pursed lips, breath out slowly (Imagine you were cooling a cup of hot Tea!) Let your whole body become loose and relaxed.

Repeat this 8-10 times. After you have completed the sequence give yourself a few minutes to reflect on how relaxed you feel at that moment.

Anger!

"Do not teach your children never to be angry; teach them how to be angry"

Lyman Abbott

There's nothing wrong with being angry it's an emotion we all share and one we can all relate to. We simply can't avoid it, it's all around us. All we have to do is switch on the TV or open a Newspaper to see its results. Whether it is in the news or a part of a gripping storyline on our favourite show anger is there. It's very similar to stress in the sense that it also has a 'fight' or 'flight' response which I mentioned in the previous chapter. It can be either positive or negative depending on how we respond to it. Again, it's a personal emotion and what might make one person angry maybe water off a ducks back to another! The positive side of anger is simple; it helps us recognise the issues or situations around us that we don't like and gives us motivation to do something about it. However, violence, verbal abuse and aggression are all very negative responses that can ruin lives and often prevent us living happily and healthily.

When was the last time you were angry? How did it make you feel? Did you do anything about it? How did you deal with it?

My mom sat me down one day and announced that she and my Stepdad were separating and that we were moving away. I wasn't surprised that they were separating as I'd sensed they were having problems but I was shocked by the moving away part. Why should we have to move? What about school? What about my friends? I wondered if she had given any of those things a thought at all. At that point she forgot to mention we weren't just moving down the road but to a completely different town. She decided to tell me that part during a visit to McDonalds which in itself was a little suspect as we had never visited McDonalds on a week day. Unfortunately for her my reaction wasn't quite what she was expecting, not in a public place anyway! I got mad and told her straight that I wasn't going. Over the course of a week I tried everything I could to prevent the move. I ran away (only got as far as the neighbours) I cried and pleaded to family members to talk some sense into her and even though they were sympathetic there was nothing they could do. I was really close to my Grandparents and spent a lot of time at their house. It was where everyone in the family got together and probably the only time I got to spend time with my cousins. This announcement felt like a nightmare... the worst kind.

On the day I arrived at my new home for the first time I felt sad and angry and those feelings took over my whole body. The move had taken place during the School holidays and I had spent two fun filled weeks with my Dad so I hadn't really had time to think about it too much. My mum had obviously been busy as the house was newly decorated and my room was arranged exactly the way I liked it. I could see my mum was happy so I tried really hard not to seem ungrateful but the only thing I could think about was the fact that I had this lovely new bedroom but no friends to play with and no one to talk to. I felt alone and out of place i just wanted my old room, in my old house, with my old friends. I was missing familiar sounds too. We had previously lived on an estate so it was quite noisy dogs barking, car alarms sounding or simply children playing were sounds I was used to they made me feel safe. But now it was different because it was quiet and I hated it. We spent a few weeks getting the house just the way we liked it and before I knew it I was starting a new school and mom had a new job.

My first day at school was the longest day of my life. Everyone was friendly enough but nothing like the people I had left behind. I spent weeks trying to find someone I could relate to or at least something to help shake off the feeling of anger I had deep down inside. I felt like a volcano on the verge of erupting and I couldn't do anything about it. I had no one to talk to and everyone and everything got on my nerves. Whenever anyone tried to talk to me I would simply shrug my shoulders or give no more than two word responses. I could see by their expressions that they were fed up with my attitude but I didn't care because as far as I was concerned I didn't want to be there. After two months I still hadn't made any friends and I had hardly spoken to my family this fuelled my anger. Why did I have to move? Why didn't my stepdad move away instead? Why didn't my dad fight for me? These thoughts taunted me every single day. Every time I tried talking to my mom about it I would stop myself as I could see how happy she was. Unfortunately it wasn't long before my Volcano erupted and it happened at school during a lesson. It was the day our teacher decided to separate the class into groups of four. We had to design a map for a treasure hunt as we were learning about pirates. I had suggested we make card board cut outs and stick them on the paper for effect but the others wanted to draw images straight onto the paper. I sensed that because I was the new girl no matter what I had suggested they would have disagreed with it so I reacted. I picked up a pen and scribbled over every inch of the work they had done. You can imagine their response, complete disgust. The teacher sent me to see the headmaster and that was the first of many visits to the Headmasters office. I spent on average two days a week there and this went on for weeks. I would promise it wouldn't happen again and at the time I meant it but I would be back there a few days later. If I wasn't being punished for the acts of violence I displayed towards fellow pupils, it was for the verbal abuse towards the teachers. I didn't recognise myself during those episodes; in fact, I was rather ashamed of my actions and deeply hurt by the misery they caused. My mum was so upset she didn't know what to do and she couldn't understand why I was so angry. The Head Master had even threatened me with suspension as I was running out of chances. Then one day something changed. A teacher from the year above was taking our class because our usual teacher was off sick. She complimented me on my handwriting and creative writing and she suggested I take part in her calligraphy classes that she held once a week after school. I wasn't sure what calligraphy was but I knew it involved some kind of handwriting so I accepted the offer there and then.

The Calligraphy teacher was a tall, brunette, elegant lady who spoke with a soft caring voice. She reminded me of a Ballerina; she seemed to have a colourful presence about her. The way she explained things to me made immediate sense. I became instantly involved. I looked forward to her lessons they became the highlight of my week. I often walked home after school by myself but if my mum was to working I would stay behind and help the teacher clean up as I hated being in the house alone. The teacher and I would talk about all kinds of things. She told me she had two children, a husband and two cats and I told her about my life before I had moved. She was so easy to talk to and I had a lot to say. It was nice to get everything off my chest; but despite the teachers' good intention the issue that caused the anger in the first place still remained. Thanks to her I was able to place my energies into something creative. She showed me that getting angry and upset was a normal reaction but the way I was expressing my anger was inappropriate and it was getting in the way of my studies and making friends and she was right. I had spent so much time sitting outside the headmaster's office that I was missing important lessons. I eventually began taking part in other after school activities such as netball, hockey and athletics. I gradually made friends, some of which I still talk to today so I guess it worked out ok in the end.

Don't get me wrong my anger issues stayed with me for a while but I found appropriate ways of venting them until they eventually disappeared. This experience taught me how to deal with anger more appropriately. I learnt so much from that situation. It taught me that the immediate effects of anger can have an appropriate and inappropriate effect; lashing out, being abusive and violent achieves nothing. In the long term can not only affect your health but the relationships you have with family and friends. Who wants to be around someone who has violent angry outbursts? This is therefore INAPPROPRIATE responses.

Here's another example; I was recently caught up in a traffic jam. It was literally stop, start, stop, and start for nearly half an hour. Everybody was probably a little annoyed and anxious after all, no one likes waiting at the best of times! Unfortunately for one man the wait got too much for him to handle. He started tooting his horn, shouting verbal abuse out of his window and too be honest he made matters far worse. In the end the man in the car in front became angry at the way he was reacting and decided to get out of his car. Let's just say that in the end the situation had to be defused by the Police which caused more of a delay and ultimately solved nothing.

 A person who doesn't at least try and manage their anger effectively runs the risk of not only living a life where situations are unnecessarily blown out of proportion but also one that prevents happiness.

Why not try……

Because anger can cloud our judgement it can often lead us to making decisions we regret and rational thinking goes completely out of the window. After an angry outburst we make excuses "I only did that because I was angry" or "that would never have happened if you hadn't made me mad" These are both excuses and not solutions.

As I said, anger is a normal emotion but it becomes a big problem if you can't control it.

Do you get angry quickly?

Do you find that you get annoyed by everyday inconveniences?

Does this often lead to violent outburst?

Do you dwell on situations for a long time that make you angry?

If you have answered yes to any of the above questions you need to manage your anger. This can be done in many effective ways. Here are a short list of methods you may find useful;

1. Take a deep breath, step away from the situation and ask yourself "why am I really mad?" You may come to the conclusion that the anger is misdirected.

2. Make a conscious effort to stay away from situations or even people that stir angry feelings.

3. Be on time. Often angry situations can occur from bad time management.

4. Regular exercise is an excellent way to de-stress the body and mind. People who exercise regularly tend not to over react.

5. Talking to someone instead of reacting can often put a situation into perspective. Because anger makes us irrational talking can diffuse the angry situation.

A positive attitude

Right now I can honestly say that I am the happiest I have ever been and I am truly blessed. I am also fortunate to be surrounded by some pretty amazing people. I now have the career that I love and I have a lot to look forward to. But you know what? I feel this way because I choose to and not because of my circumstances. I made a choice a long time ago to appreciate all aspects of my life, even the bad times! You're probably wondering why anyone would want to appreciate the bad times. Well, I came to realise that my attitude played a huge part in my happiness. This realisation came to me after a series of 'bad patches'.

A few years ago I was extremely unhappy. This wasn't down to one thing in particular; it was more to do with the fact that a number of things were just not going the way I wanted them to. Within a 12 month period I'd broken up with my partner and had to move house, I was in a job I hated and I was in a lot of debt. Everyday I would wake up with no enthusiasm for life and nothing to look forward to. Whenever I tried to explain how I was feeling I was always told to 'cheer up' but how? It's a lot easier said than done when you're feeling low.

One evening I was on the bus making my way home from work and a lady sat next to me. I wasn't usually one for having conversations with strangers but I took an instant liking to her. We engaged in a bit of small talk at first and then she told me how her husband had just suffered a stroke and that her son had recently passed away leaving his wife and new born baby behind. Not only was she caring for her bed ridden husband but she was also on her way to see her new Grandson who looked remarkably like her deceased son. Just when I thought her life seemed full enough she then went on to tell me that she also volunteered twice a week at a homeless centre. As I sat there and listened to this complete stranger giving me detailed accounts of her life, I honestly felt bad. I couldn't believe how strong she was. I mean, what was I complaining about? When I asked her how she coped she said 'you've got to stay positive and give thanks for the things you do have rather than complain and worry about the things you don't have because life is too short' as soon she said it I knew it was time for me to change. What she said had a profound effect on me as those words will stay with me forever because she was right. Here was this woman who had not only experienced losing her only child and nursing her sick husband back to health but she managed to stay positive. I felt so motivated by her and spent months afterwards working on my thoughts which were far too negative.

The first thing I had to change was how I felt about my job. I wasn't happy there but I knew that with the experience I had gained from the company along with my qualifications there was nothing stopping me from looking for another one. Instead of going to work with a negative attitude I started working on a positive one. I stopped blaming other people or the situations, my bad attitude and my depression. I began to totally restructure my whole way of thinking and took full responsibility for my life. I was so determined not to slip back into my old ways of negative thinking that I placed a 'post-it' note on my wall beside my bed with the words;' **I am grateful, I am blessed and I am happy'** and I drew a big smiley face on it. I would read this out loud every morning and every night before I went to bed. After a while I found the words helpful and empowering. I discovered much later on that using such positive words in this way is called an 'Affirmation'.

An affirmation can be described as a declaration that something is true. If we hold a particular thought or belief for a long time we begin to act on that thought whether positive or negative. Repeating a positive affirmation on a daily basis can change negative thoughts, beliefs and attitudes. It isn't an easy task; a negative thought tends to carry more weight than those that are positive. It's easier to look at life and even the world through a negative lens;

we complain, we judge, we get stressed and angry which are all very negative responses to situations but one's that can be changed over time. It may take some time to understand this but the sooner you begin the easier it will be to make those changes. If you're not convinced then try looking at it like this; imagine for a second that someone you know tells you you're not good enough, they tell you this everyday and the words go around in your head. You feel low, depressed and you begin to believe it. As a result of believing someone else's beliefs you begin to act, think and behave like a person who just isn't good enough. Now let's look at the flip side, let's say you tell yourself that you ARE in fact good enough and capable of achieving many great things. If you repeat this everyday and those words go round in your head and you eventually begin to believe it and the negative self talk dies of starvation. So what happens then? Yes you've got it; you being to act, think and behave like someone who is not only good enough but has the capability of achieving great things. I rest my case!

As we think, so we become......

"The thought manifests the word, the word manifests as the deed, the deed develops into habit and the habit hardens in character, so watch the thought and it's very ways with care, and let it spring from love born out of concern for all beings, as the shadow follows the body . As we think, so we become"

Buddha -from the Dhaammapad

Where do our attitudes come from

Your personality;   Your personality is who you really are deep down inside. Your attitudes influence who you are and are also an aspect of your personality.

Your environment: Your surroundings can have a huge effect on your attitude. If you were brought up in a poor neighborhood for example, this could prevent you from striving for success or it could be the thing that stops you even trying and giving up easily.

Your 'self' image: Yourself image is how you see yourself. If you have a negative opinion of yourself then everything around you can seem negative too.

Your beliefs: The thoughts that you hold influence your attitude the most. So if your beliefs are negative then your attitude becomes negative too.

Your associations: If you spend a lot of time around people who have negative attitudes or beliefs, then it would be quite easy for those beliefs and attitudes to rub off on you.

The choices you make: Your attitude is something you control. If you wish to change it, then that is your choice. Because your attitude is one that you decide to carry with you, then ultimately you decide whether it is a positive or a negative one.

Taking responsibility for your actions: Taking full responsibility for your actions is not a sign of weakness it is in fact it is a sign of maturity, strength and courage. A person who can hold their hands up and own what they have done is one who accepts that actions have consequences, whether they it be good or bad. Having this type of attitude in is not only empowering but it is also one that earns respect.

Why not try......

Developing a positive attitude is not an easy task especially considering the pressures our daily lives can bring. But despite this, if you decide to have a positive attitude you choose a life filled with happiness, healthy relationships, self confidence and much more.

Here are a few useful exercises to help you get started;

1) Don't let anyone else's negative attitude influence yours. If a positive attitude is what you truly desire, try and avoid people who are unsupportive.

2) Pay attention to what you are thinking. Because you are probably more likely to have more negative thoughts than positive ones, as soon as a negative thought comes into your head try and replace it with a positive one.

3) Make a list of the list of things you want to change. Include your thoughts and feelings, even the bad ones.....then take action!

4) Get into the habit of positive self-talking everyday. For example, 'I am happy and healthy' or 'each day, things are getting better and better'.

5) Apologise if you have made a mistake. Taking responsibility for your actions puts you in control of your life. You are the captain of your own ship.......own it!! It's a healthy attitude to have.

A positive attitude is making sure your mind is guiding you towards your goals and dreams. Not only that but motivation, healthy relationships, overcoming stress, fear and anger and all the subjects covered in this book can easily be achieved with a positive attitude.

Confidence

Are you confident? Are you the type of person who is capable of achieving your goals? Do you set out to do something but lack of confidence holds you back? Do you know that it is possible to be confident in some areas and lack it in others? Whether or not you have it at any given time depends on how you view it. Did you know that confidence is something that can be built upon? Yes it's true! This is because confidence often relates to your own thoughts and beliefs. Those beliefs affect the way you think and respond. We all tend to be self critical and what we believe deep down inside our minds can affect how you see ourselves. If we have a negative opinion about ourselves we tend to see things in a negative light. This is not an empowering state of mind. First of all I want to point out to you that **NOBODY IS PERFECT!** Secondly I want you learn how to love, appreciate and accept who you are with and without your faults. I'm not talking about vanity either I'm talking about having the type of connection with yourself where you trust your own feelings, trust your own thoughts and trust that whatever decisions you make are YOURS. Having that kind of connection with yourself inspires confidence and the ability to achieve the goals you have set for yourself. It is also a great way of coming to terms with both your strengths and weaknesses.

If you have achieved anything in the past you will almost certainly continue to achieve. If your lack of confidence is backed by fear then please re-read the Chapter about fear and evaluate what it is you are really afraid of. We all have times in our lives where we are faced with challenges and new adventures which take us out of our comfort zone. This is where confidence can be challenged and we begin to question our abilities. But you know what? It is perfectly normal. I am sure that if you were to ask your parents, teachers or friends they would tell you that they too have had confidence issues.

I would have described myself as a confident person, I was confident about being confident! The first time I really had to question it was on my first day at University. I sat in the car park for atleast 20 minutes questioning why the hell I was there!! My confidence was nowhere to be found. I sat in my car convinced that it was a mistake. I began asking myself 'how could someone like me, a single mom, go to university? Was I kidding myself? Was I good enough?' I then began to reflecting back on how great it felt telling all my family and friends that I was going to University. I also thought about how great I would feel actually graduating and having a degree! I spent a few moments collecting my thoughts. I told myself 'yes you can, yes you can' and I repeated those words in my head for most of that day and you know what? It eventually worked! I was nervous but I decided from that moment on that if I could get through it I could do anything. Since then my confidence has been knocked on numerous occasions and it always seems to come into question when I am venturing into something new. A recent example is when I was asked to do a talk to a small group of women about the trials and tribulations of being a young mum. My first thought was *' why would anyone be interested in what I have to say?'* and *'I can't talk in front of strangers, I'll look stupid!'* I then began to list in my mind the reasons why I shouldn't do it. That's when it hit me; this was actually what I wanted. Public speaking was the next step toward my ultimate goal. Those feelings of doubt, fear and self criticism were replaced with an over whelming feeling of pride and accomplishment. I then decided that the only way I would go through with it was to plan. So I set to work. Firstly I began with the positive attitude that I would give the best talk I possibly could. Secondly I worked out what I wanted to say and how I was going to say it. By planning ahead and preparing myself I made myself feel that little bit more confident. On the days building up to my appearance I decided to focus on the reason why I was doing it and this helped me on the big day. I had mentally prepared myself and stayed focused and it fortunately it went well. The fact that a few minor things did go wrong during my presentation was manageable. The minor hitches actually brought a bit humor to the topic and it showed my audience that I was only human and not perfect. I am now looking forward to doing it again.

The moral of the story is this; the more and more you push yourself into going the extra mile, the more and more you build your self confidence. Your self confidence will be the very thing that stands in the way of your success and you owe it to yourself to challenge and motivate yourself to just **DO IT!** And why?.... Because **YOU CAN!**

Why not try......

Lack of self confidence is not uncommon but it may present a problem for you if it prevents you from achieving your goals and living the life you truly desire. Trusting in your own abilities is empowering and inspiring especially to those around you who may look to you for guidance. On the flip side, lack of trust in your abilities can keep you stuck in a mental state of fear. As we have already uncovered fear can often stop us in our tracks and become a major obstacle.

To unleash your true potential if you are ever confronted with confidence issues why not try using one or more of the following exercises.

1. Take on the attitude of 'YES I CAN' this is a great boost for your confidence. You can say it out loud or to yourself and feel free to say it as many times as you like. Eventually it will replace the attitude of 'NO I CAN'T'

2. Make a list of all your best accomplishments and all the things you are good at. Once completed I want you to read what you have written and when you have read through it I want you to

compliment yourself, that's right, give yourself a round of applause! If you had accomplished something once, twice, three time etc you can do it again!

3. Make plans! If you have to step outside your comfort zone, plan ahead. Be on time and Plan your journey. If you're going somewhere you haven't been to before allow plenty of time (just in case) being stressed is not going help.

4. Deep breathing; Taking deep breaths calms your nerves and it helps in situations where your mind gets the better of you. Deep relaxed breathing is associated with calm, confidence and security. Short quicker breaths are associated with stress and fear. Practicing deep breathing when those fears and feelings arise will help to reduce the impact they have on your self-confidence.

Remember NOBODY is perfect. Striving to be perfect is only going to limit you and your achievements. Accept yourself for who you are despite your flaws. Being aware of your strengths and weaknesses inspires confidence.

Knowing yourself better than anyone else is the foundation from which all you desire will grow.

Positive Affirmations...

Today is going to be a great day!

I am beautiful, intelligent, confident and strong!

I am truly blessed and grateful!

I am a magnet. I attract success, happiness and love!

Everyday in every way my life is getting better!

I can achieve anything I put my mind to!

I am at peace with my past and choose to move forward, happily and joyfully!

I am grateful for all the wonderful things I have in my life and look forward to receiving more!

I create my own happiness!

I am happy and healthy!

I am calm and relaxed in every situation.

God is always a good God, I have faith in him and he gives me strength!

Yes!!! I can do it!

I believe in myself even if those around me do not!

If you're feeling down read through the list. Pick one that appeals to you or you can make up your own, read them/it out loud. Repeat this 10 times or more each morning and night. After doing this I not only want you to feel how empowering these words can be but I want you to remember what I said at the beginning of the book which is; that you are a special gift and someone worth knowing. Believe in yourself and the rest will follow.

My Final thought

To dream and to aspire is a part of who we are but our motivation can often be lost or held down by outside forces. People, situations and circumstances can steer us in directions we really do not want to go in. I hope that you take the time to explore your true potential and think about who you really are. I also hope that you are happy and confident that no matter what; *you are special and loved*!!!!

All the best,

Michelle x

"The purpose of learning is growth and our minds, unlike our bodies, can continue growing as we continue to live"

Mortimer Alder

I found this Book very stimulating and thought provoking. I feel that the young people will benefit from it. It will inspire them to think differently and encourage them to make different choices. It certainly gave me food for thought, thanks Michelle!

Natasha Fleming. Probation Officer, West Midlands.

Having read through this Book I can see through my own experiences as a GP how such a Book on the relevant issues would be beneficial to the developing youth of today. This Book will provide the reader with knowledge, guidance and tools to create a happier life. It will also give them an insight into the benefits of Self Awareness.

Dr Rousseau. South London.

I would definitely use this Book as a guide in my workshops. The great combination of real life stories and information makes it an appealing, interesting and informative read. I really enjoyed it.

Rick Frost. CEO of Frosted Ice Inc. Pride of Britain and MOBO award winner 2008.

Printed in Great Britain
by Amazon